Original title:
Embracing Emotional Echoes

Copyright © 2024 Swan Charm
All rights reserved.

Author: Sabrina Sarvik
ISBN HARDBACK: 978-9916-86-611-5
ISBN PAPERBACK: 978-9916-86-612-2
ISBN EBOOK: 978-9916-86-613-9

The Impact of Fleeting Glances

A glance shared in passing light,
A spark ignites, a heart takes flight.
In that brief moment, worlds collide,
Silent whispers, feelings abide.

Eyes that meet, yet quickly roam,
Promises whispered, far from home.
In shadows cast, intentions sway,
A fleeting glance that shifts the day.

Fables of the Fractured Spirit

In stories told of hearts that break,
Fractured spirits, dreams at stake.
Each tale weaves sorrow, joy entwined,
Lessons learned, but hard to find.

Through the seams, the sunlight streams,
Mending hearts with fragile beams.
Fables echo through the years,
In whispered truths and hidden fears.

Dances with the Fleeting Moments

Moments drift like leaves in air,
A dance of time, both fine and rare.
Each heartbeat marks the step we take,
In rhythm with the choices we make.

Twirl and sway in life's embrace,
Find the beauty in the chase.
As laughter fades, a memory stays,
In fleeting moments, we find our ways.

Traces of Yesterday's Happiness

In corners dark, the memories dwell,
Traces of joy, a wistful spell.
Photographs breathe life anew,
Echoing laughter, shades of blue.

Yesterday's dreams, like flowers bloom,
Filling the heart with sweet perfume.
In every smile, a story lies,
Traces of joy beneath the skies.

The Elegant Sigh of Memories Past

In twilight soft, the shadows creep,
Whispers of dreams that gently sleep.
Faint laughter dances on the breeze,
Time holds its breath, a moment seized.

Faded photographs, colors worn,
Softly they speak of love reborn.
Each glance a thread, a tale to weave,
In hearts entwined, we still believe.

Ripples of joy in a quiet stream,
Fragments of life, a cherished dream.
Through the haze of what once was near,
Echoes of laughter shimmer clear.

A candle flickers, shadows play,
Illuminating paths of yesterday.
In silence, time begins to mend,
The elegant sighs, our hearts transcend.

With every heartbeat, stories spun,
In the embrace of love, we run.
Memories dance like leaves in fall,
In the gentle sigh, we hear them call.

Canvases of Unfolding Echoes

In the gallery of time, we stand,
Colors swirling, a painter's hand.
Each stroke a heartbeat, vivid and bold,
Stories unfolding, secrets told.

Whispers of light on the canvas bright,
Capturing dreams in the fading light.
The brush of desire, swift and free,
Sketches of moments meant to be.

Textures of laughter, shadows of pain,
Layered emotions, a sweet refrain.
In the silence between each hue,
Life's echoes linger, firm and true.

Frames of memory, worn at the edges,
Gardens of hope in pastel hedges.
The artist's vision, a portal wide,
Canvases of time, where dreams abide.

With every heartbeat, a splash of grace,
Exploring the depths of this sacred space.
In the gallery's arms, we will find,
The echoes of life, beautifully entwined.

The Dance of Echoing Dreams

In twilight's hush, whispers sway,
Shadows intertwine, fading away.
Stars above twinkle with glee,
Embracing the night, wild and free.

Through valleys of silence, echoes roam,
Carrying secrets of a forgotten home.
Each heartbeat matches the timeless tune,
As dreams awaken beneath the moon.

Gentle breezes brush the trees,
Swaying in rhythm, drifting with ease.
Fragments of laughter fill the air,
Inviting the night to linger there.

With every step, the world sways slow,
In dances of stories only they know.
Beneath the glow of a silver beam,
They twirl together in a waking dream.

And when the dawn draws near their flight,
They'll leave behind the whispers of night.
Yet in the heart, they'll always stay,
Echoes of dreams that softly sway.

Murmurs Beneath a Starlit Sky

Soft winds carry secrets untold,
Through whispers of night, in dreams bold.
Moonbeams cast a gentle glow,
On lovers who wander, hearts aglow.

The universe sings a lullaby sweet,
Where earth and cosmos silently meet.
Each twinkle above, a nod so near,
As hearts pulse in rhythm, devoid of fear.

Under the vastness, they seek to find,
Murmurs of fate, intertwined.
With hopes and wishes, they cast their lines,
In the depths of solace, their spirit shines.

Every star holds a tale sublime,
Echoing love through the folds of time.
Embracing the night, they softly sigh,
As the world beneath hears their gentle cry.

Together they weave, a tapestry bright,
With threads of stardust, heart's delight.
Beneath the sky, they lose all track,
Murmurs of love lead them back.

Heartstrings of Wistful Yearning

In the quiet corners of soft night,
Yearning echoes take gentle flight.
Heartstrings tugged by memories old,
Stories of love in whispers told.

Each glance a promise, fleeting yet true,
Moments of magic shared by just two.
Between the breaths, a longing glows,
In shadows where the sweet sorrow flows.

Wistful dreams ride on the breeze,
While time stands still, eager to please.
Beneath the stars, hope gently sways,
In the dance of longing, a sweet malaise.

Fingers trace paths of the unfulfilled,
With every sigh, a heart's desire stilled.
Yet in the ache, a beauty derived,
From the bittersweet notes of love that survived.

In silence, they find the thread that binds,
Their souls entwined in gentle winds.
A melody lingers, soft and near,
The heartstrings hum with a silent cheer.

The Language of Lost Emotions

In shadows of a past not far,
Lost emotions wander like a star.
Fragments of words, whispers of pain,
Echoes of love through memory's rain.

The heart speaks softly, yet loud in its way,
With each silent sigh, it learns to sway.
In the twilight glow of forgotten time,
The language of loss begins to rhyme.

Every tear carries tales unspoken,
In the silence lingers, promises broken.
Yet in each heartbeat, remnants remain,
Footprints of joy, shadows of pain.

Old photographs capture the light,
Moments preserved, both dark and bright.
Within every glance, a story concealed,
In the language of emotions, fate revealed.

And as the dawn chases shadows away,
The heart learns to cherish, yearn, and stay.
For in lost emotions, a truth will rise,
A melody woven beneath the skies.

The Silent Sonata of Our Lives

In quiet rooms where whispers dwell,
We play a tune only hearts can tell.
Notes of laughter, echoes of tears,
In the stillness, we face our fears.

Each moment sways, a gentle dance,
We find our rhythm in swift glance.
Silent sonatas, in shadows cast,
We weave our dreams, both slow and fast.

Time drifts like leaves on autumn streams,
Each heartbeat sings of unguarded dreams.
In the silence, we seek the light,
Guided by stars that shine at night.

Together we rise, in harmony's grace,
Finding our strength in this sacred space.
Though words may fade, the music stays,
An eternal melody, through all our days.

So let the sonata play on and on,
In the fabric of life, we'll never be gone.
For in every silence, love will abide,
A beautiful song that will never hide.

Threads of Connection in the Dark

In shadows deep where silence reigns,
We find our way through hidden pains.
Threads of connection, fragile yet strong,
Binding us gently, where we belong.

A whisper shared, a knowing glance,
In the darkness, we dare to dance.
Hearts intertwined, we chase the light,
Finding warmth in the cold of night.

Stories woven like silk on skin,
In quiet moments, we let love in.
The tapestry glimmers, secrets unfold,
In the dark, our truths are told.

Through pain and joy, we weave the tale,
Together we rise, together we sail.
Invisible threads, pulling us near,
In the dark, love vanishes fear.

So let us embrace the night with grace,
For in shadows, we find our place.
Threads of connection shall never sever,
In the dark, we are bound forever.

Echoes in the Empty Chamber

In the hall where silence lies,
Echoes linger, bittersweet sighs.
Memories dance on forgotten air,
Whispers of love, of moments rare.

Walls remember the joys we've known,
Laughter once bright, now overgrown.
Each shadow flickers, a fleeting glance,
In this chamber, we still find chance.

Time might fade, but echoes remain,
A haunting melody of love and pain.
In the emptiness, we hear the call,
Of the heartbeats that once filled the hall.

So we stand in the quiet space,
Revealing secrets, no need to brace.
In the depths of silence, we'll find our way,
In echoes, we cherish yesterday.

For in this chamber of ghosts and dust,
We find the strength that we can trust.
Though empty it seems, our spirits rise,
In echoes, the past forever ties.

The Breath of Forgotten Wishes

In twilight's hush, where dreams take flight,
We breathe in hope, emerging light.
Forgotten wishes, lost in the breeze,
Drift like petals from ancient trees.

Each whispered thought, a silent prayer,
Yearning for change, a subtle dare.
In the stillness, we seek the spark,
A glow ignites within the dark.

Longing hearts mend with gentle sighs,
As time reveals the hidden ties.
With every breath, we forge anew,
A tapestry woven, me and you.

So let the wishes rise and soar,
From quiet depths toward distant shores.
In every sigh, a promise made,
A symphony of dreams displayed.

For the breath of forgotten wishes remains,
A river of hope in love's sweet chains.
In every heartbeat, a world awaits,
Within each wish, life's magic creates.

Tides that Wash Away Regrets

The tides roll in, gentle and slow,
Songs of the sea whisper and flow.
Regrets like seashells lost in the sand,
Surrendered to waves, washed from the land.

Moonlight dances on the surface bright,
Cleansing the sorrows, bringing the light.
Each ebb and flow, a chance to release,
With every tide, we find our peace.

Drifting dreams float far from the shore,
Leaving behind what we can't restore.
Lessons learnt from the depths of the blue,
Tides wash away, they start anew.

Embrace the dawn with a heart unchained,
Hope cradled softly, not estranged.
The ocean sings to our wandering souls,
In its rhythm, the past consoles.

So let the waves take what weighs you down,
Dance in the foam, shed off your frown.
Tides that wash hold promise and grace,
A chance to rebuild, a new embrace.

The Burden of Beautiful Remnants

In corners of rooms, echoes remain,
Whispers of love, shadows of pain.
Beautiful remnants of lives long past,
Memories woven, eternally cast.

Dust on the shelves holds stories untold,
Fragments of laughter, the warmth of the cold.
Pictures of faces that fade with the years,
Captured in moments, a dance through their tears.

The burden of beauty, heavy yet light,
Balancing grief with the joy of the night.
In every treasure, a part of our heart,
And in each goodbye, a bittersweet start.

Table set for ghosts, candles aglow,
Life's fleeting essence, a soft ebb and flow.
Holding the past with a delicate touch,
Savoring memories, oh, how we clutch.

Remnants remind us of what we once knew,
A patchwork of time, both gentle and true.
In the burden of beauty, we find our way,
Through the remnants of night, we greet the day.

A Journey Through Forgotten Faces

Through dusty streets, where shadows play,
Forgotten faces drift in the gray.
Each brick and stone tells tales of old,
Of dreams and fears, of hearts that were bold.

In the silence lingers a soft refrain,
Of voices once vibrant, now faint with pain.
Journeys taken, paths untraveled,
In memory's garden, gently unraveled.

Faces of strangers, yet familiar too,
Mirrors of selves we thought we once knew.
Each glance exchanged, a fleeting embrace,
In the echoes of time, we search for a place.

Ancient whispers guide the lost souls,
Through arches and alleys, where time unfolds.
Stories of sorrow, laughter, and grace,
In every ruin, a trace of their pace.

We walk through the past, hand in hand with dreams,
Collecting the fragments, sewing the seams.
A journey through faces, both distant and near,
In the tapestry woven, we find our way clear.

Paths of Heritage Beneath Our Feet

Beneath our feet, the stories lie,
Paths of heritage, where echoes sigh.
Every step taken, a bond to the past,
In the soil of ages, memories cast.

Fingers touch earth, rich and profound,
Whispers of ancestors linger around.
In fields of courage, where dreams took flight,
We walk through the shadows, guided by light.

The songs of our kin still linger in air,
In the warmth of the sun, their love we share.
Roots intertwine in a tapestry grand,
Connections unbroken, a timeless strand.

Through valleys and hills, our lineage flows,
Each path we tread, a symphony grows.
Carving our names in the heart of this land,
We honor the journeys of those who stand.

Heritage whispers in wind and in trees,
Guiding our hearts with gentle degrees.
Paths beneath feet, a blessing bestowed,
In the dance of the past, our spirits are flowed.

The Tapestry of Timeless Tides

In the embrace of endless seas,
Waves whisper tales of ancient shores,
Underneath the silver moon's light,
Time weaves through countless hours.

Each tide a thread, a story spun,
Flowing with dreams that swiftly fade,
Cradled by the ocean's gentle hand,
Life's pattern in a dance displayed.

Seashells murmuring secrets past,
Cast upon the grains of sand,
Ebb and flow, what truth do we seek,
In this vast and shifting land?

With every surge, a memory lost,
Yet something new is born and thrives,
Connections forged in salt and foam,
In the tapestry, the soul survives.

So let the tides come pull and push,
For in their rhythm, we find peace,
A journey woven through the waves,
Where all our fears and hopes release.

Silence That Speaks Volumes

In the quiet of an empty room,
Whispers linger in the air,
Thoughts sway like shadows on walls,
In silence, we find what's rare.

A gaze that holds a thousand words,
Lost within a moment's grasp,
Echoes of what's left unspoken,
In stillness, questions start to clasp.

Hearts converse without a sound,
Yet pulses race with hidden fears,
In that hush, connections bloom,
An understanding that nears.

Time stretches, like a breath held tight,
Drawn into the quiet thread,
Where feelings weave a tapestry,
Of words that linger, yet are led.

So let the silence hold its weight,
A canvas painted with the soul,
For in the quiet, life unfolds,
And speaks of truths that make us whole.

Mosaics of Melancholy

Shattered pieces of the past,
Scattered like autumn leaves,
Each fragment holds a story told,
A mix of joy and deep reprieves.

In shades of gray, the colors blend,
A sorrowed palette weaves a song,
With every tear, a memory shines,
In this mosaic, we belong.

Forgotten dreams that haunt the night,
Covered by a blanket of stars,
Yet beauty lies in every crack,
Amidst the wounds, we heal our scars.

Like ancient art, we paint our pain,
Transforming hurt to strength anew,
In every shard, a glimpse of hope,
A journey of what we once knew.

So here we stand, amidst these pieces,
Crafting life from the things we've lost,
Mosaics gleaming with resilience,
In melancholy, we find our cost.

Gains and Losses of the Soul

In the tapestry of life we tread,
Gains measured by the heart's true weight,
What is cherished, often let go,
Life's dance of love and fate.

Each moment, a ledger, etched in time,
Losses taught us how to grow,
What we hold, what's cast aside,
In this realm, we learn to flow.

Dreams we clutch, with fingers tight,
Yet slip away like whispers in wind,
In every loss, a lesson learned,
For each beginning, there's an end.

Paths entwined that drift apart,
Yet shadows linger, memories stay,
In every heart, a story lives,
In joy and sorrow, love finds its way.

So let us gather all we've gained,
Embrace the scars that make us whole,
For in this journey 'round and 'round,
We discover the essence of the soul.

The Language of Unrequited Love

Silent whispers fill the air,
Each glance a stolen dare.
A heart that beats, yet stays unseen,
In shadows cast, love's ghostly sheen.

Longing lingers, sweet yet cruel,
Words unsaid, love's silent fuel.
In dreams, we dance, the hand of fate,
Yet, here we stand, in love's great wait.

Every word feels like a knife,
Carving paths through the heart of life.
The echo stretches far and wide,
In every sigh, love's quiet pride.

A touch, a breath, the world retreats,
Yet I alone feel love's defeat.
For in this game, I play too small,
Yearning for you, to love or fall.

Shall silence speak what hearts can't say?
In unrequited love, I sway.
With every beat, a tale is spun,
A language lost, yet never done.

Portraits in Emotional Hues

Canvas stretched beneath my gaze,
Colors dance, a vibrant blaze.
Brushstroke whispers of deep despair,
Yet joy emerges, layered care.

With every hue, a story told,
Bright yellows shine, but blues are bold.
Purples blend, a twilight sigh,
In every shade, a piece of why.

Moments captured, fleeting fast,
In careful strokes, emotions cast.
Fingers trace the lines of pain,
Yet hope emerges, blooms like rain.

Shades of green in life abound,
In forests deep, lost yet found.
Each portrait speaks of love and strife,
A picture painted of our life.

As daylight fades, colors collide,
In emotional hues, we confide.
Each canvas holds a fragment true,
A masterpiece of me and you.

The Calming of Chaotic Echoes

Through the noise, a silence grows,
Finding peace where chaos flows.
In the echoes, whispers blend,
A soothing balm, a gentle mend.

Waves of thought crash on the shore,
But in the depths, a tranquil core.
Breathing softens, tension fades,
In gentle ripples, calm cascades.

Flickering lights in the dark night,
Guide us home with their soft light.
Each echo carries tales of yore,
Yet in their depths, we seek for more.

Serenity found in whispered tones,
Melodies soothe our aching bones.
As we listen to the heart's refrain,
We discover peace may rise from pain.

In the storm, we stand as one,
Together basking in the sun.
The calming of chaotic echoes,
A promise woven where love grows.

Poetry of the Unseen Heart

In the shadows where feelings hide,
Words emerge, but struggle, bide.
Lines of longing, etched in air,
Poetry blooms, a secret rare.

Silent verses brush the soul,
In whispered tones, we feel it whole.
Each heartbeat writes a line unseen,
In every pause, a tranquil mean.

Between the words, the truth awaits,
Unlocking doors through love and fates.
In unseen realms, the heart takes flight,
Poetry glows, a beacon bright.

Fluttering dreams in starlit skies,
Wrap around us, soft goodbyes.
For though the heart may never speak,
In silent rhymes, our souls they seek.

In every phrase a journey starts,
Mapping pathways of unseen hearts.
In the silence, we find our part,
The poetry lives where pain departs.

Harmonies of the Haunted Past

Echoes linger in the air,
Whispers of love, lingering care.
Memories dance in twilight's haze,
A symphony of forgotten days.

Shadows weave through ancient halls,
Time stands still, as silence calls.
Each note strums a heart's refrain,
Filling the void where ghosts remain.

Laughter fades but beauty stays,
In haunted tunes, our spirits play.
With every chord, our souls entwined,
We embrace the echoes left behind.

In the twilight of our dreams,
Life is more than what it seems.
Harmonies of shadows blend,
The haunted past will never end.

Yet in the dark, there's light to find,
A solace for the aching mind.
Through haunted songs, we shall survive,
In remembrance, the heart's alive.

Beneath the Surface of Still Waters

Ripples dance on mirrored glass,
Secrets dwell where shadows pass.
Beneath the calm, the depths conceal,
All the truths we long to feel.

Silent whispers of the deep,
In the dark, the memories sleep.
Craving light that pierces night,
Searching for a flicker bright.

Fish are gliding, swift and sleek,
Fleeting visions, destiny's peek.
In stillness lies a brewing storm,
Unraveled tales, a hidden norm.

Nature hums a quiet tune,
Underneath the watching moon.
Water's embrace, soft and warm,
A cradle for the heart's alarm.

Beneath the surface, life abounds,
Echoes of life in watery bounds.
In still waters, we shall find,
The depth of love, forever kind.

Fragments of a Fractured Heart

Shattered pieces on the floor,
Love once rich, now feels poor.
Every jagged edge a scar,
A reminder of who we are.

In the silence, echoes play,
Words unspoken, slip away.
Hopes adrift on winds of grace,
Searching still for love's embrace.

Time may mend what seems so torn,
In darkness, new light is born.
Threads of fate weave tangled dreams,
Knitting back what fragile seems.

Yet the heart knows not to fear,
In every loss, a truth is clear.
Fragmented visions slowly fuse,
Healing comes when we choose to lose.

Resilience blooms in quiet sighs,
From brokenness, the spirit flies.
Embracing scars, we find our way,
Fragments awaken a brighter day.

Ghosts of Joy Unseen

In laughter's echo, shadows dance,
Moments lost in a fleeting glance.
Joy once bright now dims away,
Chasing ghosts of yesterday.

The sun's warm glow, a lover's light,
Flickers gently but feels so right.
In absence, joy begins to fade,
Countless memories softly invade.

Haunted dreams in quiet nights,
Whispers of forgotten delights.
Joy suspended in a realm apart,
A shadowed trace of a longing heart.

Yet within these echoes, we believe,
In every loss, we learn to grieve.
Ghosts of laughter, playful remains,
In our hearts, their essence reigns.

To cherish moments pure and bright,
Embrace the shadows, seek the light.
For joys unseen will always guide,
As we carry them, side by side.

Whispers of the Heart's Reverberation

In the quiet glow of night,
The whispers blend like starlit sighs.
A heartbeat echoes soft and light,
As shadows dance beneath the skies.

Gentle murmurs trace the soul,
Where dreams and wishes intertwine.
Each pulse reveals a hidden goal,
A tapestry of love divine.

In silence, secrets come alive,
With every thrum, the moments swell.
From depths of passion, feelings drive,
In whispers, tales of hearts to tell.

Beneath the moon's ethereal gaze,
The heart's soft song begins to rise.
In harmony, their voices blaze,
A symphony that never dies.

So let the whispers linger near,
A melody of joy and pain.
In each refrain, we hold what's dear,
The heart's true song, a sweet refrain.

Fragile Chords of Memory

In a dusky room, dust motes play,
Memories linger, faint and shy.
Fragile chords of yesterday,
In echoes soft, they come to fly.

A photograph, a fleeting glance,
Whispers of laughter, grace the air.
Each note a poem, a wistful chance,
To capture moments, bright and rare.

With every strum, a story weaves,
Of love once held and dreams set free.
Each fragile chord the heart perceives,
A symphony of you and me.

Through time's embrace, the shadows shift,
Yet in our minds, their light remains.
These fragile chords, a timeless gift,
Resonate with joy and pains.

So cherish notes that softly fade,
In quiet hearts, their music stays.
With gentle hands, these dreams we've laid,
Rings from the past, in bright arrays.

The Sound of Solitude's Embrace

In the stillness, silence reigns,
The sound of solitude unfolds.
A gentle kiss, a soft refrain,
As night reveals its secrets bold.

Among the stars, a whisper calls,
A balm for tired, wandering souls.
In solitude, the heart enthralls,
The echo of a dream that rolls.

Each breath, a note, in time's vast sea,
As waves of calm begin to rise.
The sound of solitude sets free,
A symphony beneath the skies.

In shadows deep, serenity,
Wraps around like a soft cocoon.
The haunting notes of harmony,
Infuse the night with a sweet tune.

So let the silence hold you tight,
A gentle dance, a tender trace.
In solitude, beneath the night,
Awakens joy in soft embrace.

Resounding Secrets Beneath the Skin

Beneath the surface, whispers pulse,
Resounding secrets yearn to speak.
In every heartbeat, feelings convulse,
A tapestry of truths unique.

Each scar a story, etched in time,
A testament to battles fought.
The skin, a map, a rhythm, a rhyme,
In silence, all that can't be bought.

Emotions swell like ocean tides,
In quietude, they begin to rise.
With every breath, no place to hide,
Resounding truths, a sweet disguise.

We wear our heartstrings like fine lace,
Each thread a thought, aching to show.
In every touch, a sacred space,
Where secrets dwell and love can grow.

So listen close to what's unvoiced,
In every glance, a world concealed.
In resonating hearts, rejoice,
The secrets shared, forever healed.

Echoes of Yesterday's Tears

Whispers linger in the night,
Fleeting shadows take their flight.
Memories soft as a sigh,
Time will hold them, by and by.

Faces fade, yet hearts remain,
Love once lost, still bears the pain.
In the silence, echoes call,
Tears of yesteryear enthrall.

Joy and sorrow intertwine,
In the quiet, souls align.
Bitter sweetness in the air,
Yesterday's burdens, hard to bear.

Fleeting moments, softly laid,
In the heart, love won't fade.
Echoes resonate, so clear,
Tears forgotten, endlessly near.

Reverie in the Halls of Silence

In the stillness, dreams awake,
Whispers tangle, the heart will break.
Shadows dance beneath the light,
Crafting stories out of night.

Voices echo, soft and low,
In the silence, thoughts can flow.
Memories weave through time and space,
In this hall, we find our place.

Invisible threads tie us tight,
Guiding hearts towards the light.
Every glance, a silent vow,
In this moment, here and now.

Halls of silence, deep and wide,
Where our secrets choose to hide.
In the reverie, we belong,
A melody, a whispered song.

The Rhythm of Forgotten Dreams

In twilight's glow, dreams softly fade,
Rhythms linger, softly played.
Whispers of what used to be,
Still resonate, hauntingly free.

Each heartbeat echoes a tune,
Underneath the silver moon.
Lost ambitions start to gleam,
In the silence, we redeem.

Fleeting visions swirl and sway,
On the edge of night and day.
Time's embrace, a gentle strain,
In forgotten dreams, we remain.

Rustling leaves sing our plight,
Carried forward into the night.
Memories dance, unseen seams,
Forever stitched in dreams of dreams.

Harmonies Crafted from Shadows

In the darkness, music grows,
Crafted gently, whispers flows.
Shadows weave their intricate art,
Harmonies that sway the heart.

Every note, a thread of night,
Painting silence with delight.
Softly falling, like the rain,
Dancing shadows mask the pain.

Light and dark in sweet embrace,
Every moment finds its place.
In the chaos, peace we find,
Harmonies of heart and mind.

In the still, the echoes play,
Guiding souls along the way.
Crafted from the depths we've known,
Shadows sing, we're not alone.

Echoing Through the Corridors of Time

Whispers linger in the air,
Footsteps trace the path we share.
Fragments of laughter softly play,
Guiding us through yesterday.

Shadows dance upon the wall,
Memories rise and gently fall.
Every echo, every sigh,
Holds a story passing by.

Glimmers of grace from days gone by,
Fleeting moments, oh, how they fly.
In the silence, voices call,
Together we rise, together we fall.

Time's embrace, a tender hold,
Tales of love and tales of old.
In these halls of dreams and time,
We find our reason; we find our rhyme.

Through the corridors, we roam,
Each heartbeat brings us closer to home.
In the past where we reside,
Echoes dwell and hearts collide.

Piecing Together Broken Memories

Fragments strewn across the floor,
Scattered pieces of what came before.
Faded colors, distant sights,
Searching for those lost delights.

A photograph with corners bent,
Each snapshot, a moment spent.
Whispers of who we used to be,
Building bridges to set us free.

Tender moments tucked away,
In the heart, they wish to stay.
Through the cracks of yesterday,
Healing wounds that seldom play.

Remembering laughter and tears,
The joys and shadows of our years.
Each recollection, a gentle guide,
Leading us where love abides.

As we piece this puzzle right,
Shadows merge into the light.
With every memory we reclaim,
A brighter future calls our name.

Vocabulary of the Treasured Past

Words unspoken, tales untold,
In the heart, their warmth we hold.
Whispers echo in the night,
Each syllable glows with light.

A lexicon of love and fears,
Glimpses of laughter, threads of tears.
Every phrase, a sacred trust,
Building bridges from the dust.

Gazing back with open eyes,
In the past, the treasure lies.
Each word, a key to open doors,
Unlocking what the spirit soars.

Moments captured in the sound,
Echoes of the lost and found.
In their resonance, we see,
The tapestry of you and me.

Through the ages, they remain,
Words of joy, words of pain.
In our stories, they entwine,
A language crafted, pure, divine.

Amidst the Silences That Bind

In the quiet, secrets dwell,
In hidden spaces, we can tell.
Threads of silence weave our fate,
In every heartbeat, love awaits.

Words unsaid, a gentle force,
Leading us along our course.
Softly linger, shadows blend,
In the stillness, we transcend.

The language of the heart unfolds,
In silence, the truth beholds.
With each pause, we come to know,
The deeper bond that starts to grow.

United in the hush we share,
Whispers echo, a sacred prayer.
In quiet moments, we align,
Finding strength in what's divine.

So embrace the silence that surrounds,
In it, the deepest love abounds.
Amidst the stillness, hearts entwined,
In the silence, solace we find.

Symphonies of Unspoken Words

In shadows soft, where whispers dwell,
A melody is born, a secret spell.
Each note a dream, each pause a sigh,
We dance in silence, you and I.

The air is thick with tales untold,
In hushed tones, our hearts unfold.
Fragile hopes on fragile strings,
A world of sound that silence brings.

Beyond the words we dare not speak,
In tender glances, truth we seek.
Harmony in the space between,
A symphony of what has been.

The echoes fade, but feelings stay,
In every heartbeat, in the fray.
Unvoiced love, a soft caress,
In unison, we find our rest.

So let the silence wrap us tight,
In its embrace, we find our light.
The symphonies of dreams will soar,
Unspoken words, forevermore.

The Pulse of Remembrance

Time ticks softly, a measured beat,
In fragile minds, where memories meet.
Each heartbeat echoes the past we held,
In quiet moments, our stories meld.

Faded photographs, laughter's trace,
Ghosts of joy in time's embrace.
Whispers of love still linger near,
In whispers soft, their voices clear.

With every tick, a life replays,
A canvas painted in vibrant ways.
Colors blend in a tender hue,
The pulse of life, both old and new.

Through shadows cast, we walk with grace,
In the echoes of a remembered space.
Time gives breath to what we miss,
In the heartbeat's song, we find our bliss.

So let the clock sing its gentle tone,
A melody of love we've known.
For in remembrance, we find our way,
The pulse of yesterday, here to stay.

Tracing the Lineage of Longing

Echoes of dreams, like footprints in sand,
Across the shores of a distant land.
Each wave a whisper, each tide a call,
Tracing the edges of want in us all.

From roots that ground us, to skies we chase,
Longing weaves through time and space.
A tapestry rich with threads of desire,
In the heart's loom, it spins with fire.

The trails of hope and the paths of pain,
In the quest for love, we rise, we wane.
Maps of the heart, etched deep within,
Guiding our souls where journeys begin.

Lost in the stories of who we've been,
Tracing the lineage, the kin within.
In every heartbeat lies a thread,
Binding the past to visions ahead.

So let us wander, let us explore,
The roots of longing, forevermore.
For in each step, we find our place,
Tracing our lineage with gentle grace.

Reflections in a Teardrop's Dance

In a teardrop's fall, a story flows,
A river of feelings, where sorrow grows.
Mirrored lights in droplets fair,
Capturing moments, a fragile prayer.

Each shimmer holds a thousand dreams,
Lost in the silence, where memory gleams.
A dance of shadows, a waltz of light,
In whispered echoes, day turns to night.

The weight of a tear, both heavy and sweet,
A testament of love, of loss, bittersweet.
In every drop, a longing to mend,
Reflections of hearts that struggle to blend.

Like raindrops falling on thirsty ground,
In their descent, our truths are found.
A dance of emotions, so gentle, so grand,
In the tender embrace of the heart's soft hand.

So let the teardrops fall like rain,
Each one a whisper of joy and pain.
For in their dance, we learn to see,
The beauty of life's fragility.

Serenade of the Solitary Heart

In quiet nights, the shadows dance,
A whisper soft, a fleeting glance.
The moonlight winks, a subtle call,
Yet solitude wraps its gentle shawl.

Through empty rooms, the echoes glide,
A heart confined, where dreams reside.
Each heartbeat sings a secret tune,
In the solitude, beneath the moon.

Waves of longing wash the shore,
With every pulse, I yearn for more.
A serenade to silence sings,
In the stillness, my spirit clings.

Hope rises like the morning dew,
Amidst the hearts that feel so few.
In this embrace of distant art,
I find the beauty of my heart.

Though the world may seem apart,
In shadows deep, I make my start.
This melody, though lone it seems,
Is woven with my silent dreams.

Ripples in the Pool of Memories

In stillness rests a tranquil lake,
Reflecting times the heart can take.
A leaf descends to kiss the glass,
And ripples dance where moments pass.

Each wave reveals a tale once told,
Of laughter shared and hearts of gold.
In echoes soft, the memories swell,
In this deep pool, I know them well.

Old whispers stirring in the night,
Bring forth the dreams that take their flight.
A shimmer fades, a shadow cast,
Yet time remains a sacred past.

In quiet depths, those images gleam,
Mirroring every whispered dream.
As ripples fade, the heart will know,
What once was lost can still bestow.

Time may flow, yet still I stand,
With cherished thoughts held in my hand.
These ripples linger, never tire,
In memory's pool, my heart's desire.

Chords of Resilience in the Overcast

Beneath the clouds, the music plays,
A symphony of muted days.
Each note a step through heavy air,
In storms of life, we learn to dare.

The strings of hope, they gently strum,
And for each beat, we still overcome.
For though the skies may seem to frown,
Our spirits rise, refuse to drown.

In shadows cast, we find our light,
With every chord, we gain our might.
Through heavy hearts, the melodies surge,
In times of grief, we learn to purge.

The rain may fall, but under haze,
We grip the strings and sing our praise.
Resilience found in every sound,
While in this chaos, love is bound.

Though clouds may loom, our notes will soar,
For in the dark, we rise once more.
In every challenge, we shall find,
The chords of life that bind our minds.

Chronicles of Lingering Light

The dawn breaks soft, a tender hue,
In golden rays, the world feels new.
A story written on the sky,
With every breath, I learn to fly.

The lingering light warms whispered dreams,
As twilight fades, the magic gleams.
With every star, a tale's begun,
In cosmic dance, we're all as one.

Through paths unknown, the shadows creep,
Yet in the night, our hopes we keep.
No matter where the journey leads,
The light within forever feeds.

Each moment cherished, time unfolds,
In chapters bright, our lives are told.
With open hearts, we face the night,
And find our way in fading light.

So here we stand, both brave and bold,
In chronicles of dreams retold.
For as the sun sets, we embrace,
The lingering light, our timeless grace.

Resonance of Past Lullabies

In shadows of twilight's fold,
Soft whispers of dreams retold,
The echoes linger in the night,
As stars adorn their twinkling light.

Memories drift like autumn leaves,
Carrying tales the heart believes,
In melodies woven with care,
They dance through the cool, crisp air.

Each note a thread of time's embrace,
A soothing balm, a warm, safe place,
Where childhood dreams forever thrive,
In silence, they come back alive.

The moon hums softly overhead,
While echoes of laughter gently spread,
Through corridors of yesteryear,
In lullabies, we hold them near.

So let the rhythm guide us home,
Through ages past where we once roamed,
In resonance, our spirits soar,
To cradle dreams forevermore.

The Spectrum of Forgotten Days

In faded hues of amber light,
Recall the warmth of golden bright,
When laughter danced through sunlit streams,
And life was woven with our dreams.

Each moment painted, brushstrokes bold,
The stories of the young and old,
In sepia tones, their magic stays,
A spectrum bright of forgotten days.

The echoes of a child at play,
In realms where innocence held sway,
With every whisper of the breeze,
The past emerges, sweet memories.

Through twilight hours and fading light,
We hold the moments, soft and bright,
For in our hearts they still remain,
A spectrum rich, a cherished chain.

So let us wander through the mist,
And gather days that we have kissed,
In colors that the heart relays,
The spectrum of our forgotten days.

Notes Carried by the Wind

Softly drifting, whispers blend,
In notes that sail, they twist and bend,
A song released from nature's hand,
Carried far to a distant land.

Beneath the branches, secrets flow,
In harmonies that gently grow,
Composing tales of time un-spun,
In every breeze, their lives are sung.

As twilight fades, the night will hum,
With tales born from the heart's own drum,
Each note a memory intertwined,
In the silken air, love is enshrined.

The world awakens, soft and clear,
With melodies we hold so dear,
In whispers that the night sends forth,
Notes carried by the wind's great worth.

So listen close, for you may find,
The songs that echo through your mind,
In every rustling leaf and sigh,
Notes carried by the wind, they fly.

In the Arms of Infinite Longing

In twilight's glow, we softly sway,
As shadows chant the end of day,
With hearts aglow in tender ties,
We seek the stars that light our skies.

A gentle thought, a silent plea,
In dreams we find our liberty,
For in the space where time is lost,
We hold our breath, no matter the cost.

The night extends, a velvet spread,
Embracing hopes not yet unsaid,
In whispered wishes softly sung,
In every heart, this love is sprung.

Through every tear, through every sigh,
Our spirits reach, they learn to fly,
For we are bound by love's sweet chain,
In infinite longing, we remain.

So gather close, my dear, my friend,
For in this moment, we transcend,
In arms that hold, through storm and song,
In the embrace of infinite longing.

The Pulse of Unspoken Words

In shadows deep, whispers play,
Silent truths drift far away.
Hearts beat soft, a secret dance,
In quiet corners, dreams enhance.

Voices linger, untold tales,
Across the night, where time prevails.
Each sigh holds a story clear,
Words unspoke, yet all can hear.

Fingers trace the air with grace,
Softened edges, a fleeting space.
Threads of thought, gently entwined,
In the silence, words defined.

Echoes rise from deep within,
In the void, where thoughts begin.
A pulse beats on, raw and bold,
Unseen stories waiting, told.

In the still, a language grows,
In every breath, the heart bestows.
The pulse of life, unspoken art,
Bridges built from soul to heart.

Wounds Wrapped in Serenity

Hidden scars beneath the skin,
In silence, battles lost, or win.
A tender touch, the balm of care,
In moments fleeting, hearts lay bare.

Calm waves break on jagged shores,
Healing whispers, life restores.
Nature's grace, a soft embrace,
Cocooned in peace, finding place.

Threads of gold in frayed designs,
Stitched with love, the heart aligns.
In twilight's glow, memories gleam,
Wounds wrapped tight, still chase the dream.

The dance of night, a gentle sigh,
Beneath the stars, we learn to fly.
A serenade, a lullaby,
Bringing hope as time goes by.

Softly, softly, moments weave,
In fragile hearts, we learn to believe.
Wrapped in stillness, pain recedes,
Serenity plants the healing seeds.

Chasing Memories Through the Mist

Veils of fog on morning's breath,
Memories linger, whispering death.
Footsteps echo down the lane,
Chasing shadows, avoiding pain.

Fragments float on ghostly streams,
In the haze, we chase our dreams.
Ghosts of laughter, bittersweet,
In the distance, hearts repeat.

Through the mist, I see your face,
Flickering light, a soft embrace.
Memories dance like shadows fleet,
In the stillness, our souls meet.

Each moment lost, a treasure found,
In whispered tales, we are bound.
Chasing echoes, soft and bright,
Through the mist, we search for light.

Time flows like a silent stream,
In every memory, a dream.
Through the fog, we navigate,
Awakening to love's sweet fate.

Cries of the Quiet Storm

Beneath the calm, a tempest waits,
Silent howls push through the gates.
Tempers churn in muted mist,
Cries unheard, in shadows twist.

Gentle rain, a whispered plea,
Thunder rolls through secrecy.
In every heart, a storm resides,
Quiet thunder, where truth hides.

Clouds collide in darkened skies,
Lightning flashes, quick goodbyes.
In stillness, chaos finds its form,
The beauty held in each quiet storm.

Every breath, a whispered shout,
In hidden spaces, fears pour out.
Hearts awake, a raging tide,
In silent cries, we must confide.

Through darkened nights, we weave our fate,
In the tempest, we navigate.
Cries of the quiet storm we bear,
In the eye, we find our share.

Lament of the Unheard

In shadows deep, they softly cry,
Voices lost as they drift by.
Silent whispers weave through night,
Seeking solace, yearning light.

Words unspoken, heavy pain,
Echoes linger, like cold rain.
Hope a flicker, dimmed and frail,
Carried forth on the wind's wail.

Chained to dreams that never bloom,
Hearts surrounded by the gloom.
Yet, in darkness, spirits rise,
Finding strength in unseen ties.

Wings of sorrow, yet they soar,
Through the silence, seek for more.
Lamentations softly blend,
In the night, they find a friend.

Each unheard cry begins to weave,
Tapestries of those who grieve.
Though the world may choose to blind,
In their hearts, the truth they find.

Chains of Fragile Laughter

A smile dances on the brink,
While shadows loom, they start to sink.
Laughter echoes, brittle sound,
But in the joy, despair is found.

Moments fleeting, like the breeze,
Hiding pain beneath the tease.
Masks of joy, but eyes reveal,
The weight of wounds that never heal.

Fragile bonds, yet tightly wound,
In this chaos, solace drowned.
Each chuckle hides a jagged scar,
Chains of laughter, yet so far.

Wishing for a gentle release,
From the struggle, seeking peace.
In the giggles, silence dwells,
Where truth lies deep in hidden wells.

So laugh we must, as shadows play,
Finding light in the gray sway.
Chains may rattle, hearts may freeze,
Yet within, we long for ease.

Serenade of the Soul's Terrain

In the depths where silence dwells,
A melody of spirit swells.
Notes like whispers kiss the air,
Painting colors, bright and rare.

Landscapes shift beneath our feet,
Journey woven with heartbeat.
Trails of memory, dust and light,
Guide us forward through the night.

Each step taken, story spun,
Beneath the moon, the world's begun.
Echoes dance on softest ground,
In this serenade, peace is found.

Voices blend—a sacred hymn,
Carving paths both wild and dim.
In the heart, a compass true,
Leading souls to something new.

So sing we now, of joy and pain,
In the echoes, love's refrain.
Journey on, with open eyes,
For in the soul, the beauty lies.

Ghosts of Joy and Sorrow

In the twilight, shadows gleam,
Ghosts of laughter haunt the dream.
Memories flicker, soft and bright,
Dancing gently in the night.

Sorrows linger, bittersweet,
Whispers tracing through the street.
Echoes of a time once grand,
Grasping tightly, grains of sand.

Joy and sorrow, hand in hand,
Woven tightly, like the strand.
Each heartbeat, both ache and bliss,
A fleeting, fragile world we miss.

Yet in the night, they softly play,
Together in their unique way.
Lessons learned from paths once crossed,
In every joy, something lost.

So let the ghosts both dance and sing,
For in their presence, we take wing.
In their laughter, we find our cheer,
In their sorrow, we shed a tear.

Flight of the Unexpressed Heart

In shadows deep, emotions hide,
A silent song, where dreams reside.
Whispers caught, in fleeting breath,
A journey marked, by quiet depth.

Each heartbeat drifts, like autumn leaves,
Carried forth on gentle eves.
Unseen wings, they yearn to soar,
To distant lands, to seek for more.

A canvas bare, of untold art,
Brush strokes soft, of fervent heart.
With every pulse, the shadows dance,
A secret realm, a whispered chance.

Echoes fade, yet still they sing,
A haunting call, from within spring.
Unexpressed, but deeply felt,
In each refrain, the heart has knelt.

Yet as we dream, the skies ignite,
With hopes that tremble in the night.
A flight begins, though words may cease,
In silent grace, we find our peace.

Eulogy for the Unsaid

In quiet halls where echoes dwell,
Reside the words we dare not tell.
With trembling hands, we bury tight,
The thoughts we keep, away from light.

Each whispered hope, a secret kept,
In shadows cast, where silence crept.
A longing sigh, a heavy heart,
In muted tones, we live apart.

A eulogy for dreams untold,
In silent grief, as memories unfold.
We mourn the moments, fleeting wise,
The stories lost, behind our eyes.

Yet in the stillness, life can gleam,
From unspoken words, a quiet dream.
Each sigh whispers, of what might be,
A life adorned in secrecy.

For in the echoes of what's unsaid,
Lives the essence we all dread.
A voice that lingers, soft yet grand,
In silent tribute, we take a stand.

The Voices that Fade

In corners dark, where shadows weave,
The voices fade, as hearts believe.
They linger soft, like morning mist,
A fleeting touch, a gentle tryst.

Once vibrant songs, now whispers pale,
As echoes drift, on autumn's trail.
These cherished sounds, once loud and clear,
Now fade away, yet draw us near.

A tapestry of fleeting tones,
In every note, a heart bemoans.
Yet in the quiet, reason reigns,
For love remains, despite the pain.

In memory's grasp, they softly glide,
Like waves that swell, then lose their tide.
Each voice a star, that fades from sight,
Yet softly shines through endless night.

Though time may dim, their essence stays,
In every heart, through silent praise.
The voices of old, though drifted away,
Will always shimmer, come what may.

Between Grief and Grace

In tears that fall, there's beauty found,
Between the sorrows, joy unbound.
A tapestry of light and shade,
Where hope emerges, fears are laid.

For every loss, a lesson's gift,
In fractured moments, spirits lift.
The heartache deep, yet love remains,
In every weep, a warmth sustains.

A dance of shadows, dusk to dawn,
In fragile breath, a strength reborn.
Between the grief, a path we trace,
To find the peace, within the grace.

With every heartbeat, we transcend,
In sorrow's touch, the soul can mend.
Embrace the now, the fleeting chance,
For life unfolds, a sacred dance.

In every tear, a story grows,
Between the lines, the heart still knows.
For out of sorrow, blossoms bloom,
Between grief and grace, there's always room.

Sifting Through Shattered Dreams

In shadows cast by hopes once bright,
We sift through fragments in the night.
Each piece a whisper, soft and small,
Echoes of dreams we dared to call.

The glimmer fades, yet we still try,
To weave together what went awry.
With weary hands, we shape and mold,
As stories linger, yet untold.

A tapestry of broken schemes,
We gather up the scattered beams.
And though the light seems far away,
We hold the spark, we find our way.

Through every tear and silent scream,
We search for solace in the dream.
In every shatter, we find a thread,
A promise of life where hopes once fled.

So here we stand, though dreams may break,
Resilient hearts will never quake.
For in despair, we learn to glean,
The strength that lies in shattered dreams.

The Glow of Embraced Shadows

In twilight's hush, where light concedes,
Shadows whisper forgotten needs.
Embraced by night, they dance and sway,
Creating warmth in their own way.

Each flicker glows with soft delight,
A tapestry of dark and light.
In silence held, they softly hum,
A lullaby of what's to come.

The moonlight weaves through leafy seams,
A silver thread in tangled dreams.
We trace the curves of whispered tales,
As night reveals where magic sails.

In shadow's realm, we find our peace,
A gentle calm, a sweet release.
The glow ignites, ignites our souls,
In darkness deep, we feel it whole.

To hold the night within our heart,
For in shadows, new dreams start.
As stars align, we learn to see,
The beauty in what sets us free.

Cacophony of Silent Sentiments

Amidst the noise of unspoken words,
A symphony of thoughts emerges,
Each silence paints a vivid scene,
In emotions felt but rarely seen.

A clash of feelings, fierce and bold,
Yet in the quiet, stories unfold.
Unraveled truths beneath the din,
We listen close to what's within.

The heart's refrain, a distant tune,
Plays softly under the silver moon.
While faces mask the storm inside,
We yearn for peace, we seek to hide.

The cacophony, a whispered call,
Of love and loss that binds us all.
Within the noise, we seek to find,
A gentle thread that's intertwined.

So here we stand, amidst the roar,
With hearts that speak what we ignore.
In silence, we can hear the sound,
Of sentiments that know no bound.

The Heart's Hidden Portrait

Within the chambers of the soul,
A canvas waits to be made whole.
A hidden portrait, brush in hand,
In colors soft, we hope to stand.

Each stroke reveals a part of us,
In vivid hues, in shades of trust.
From joy to sorrow, it all blends,
A masterpiece no eye pretends.

We paint the lines of love and pain,
In every hue, the sun and rain.
A reflection deep, a glimpse unseen,
The heart's true essence, vivid sheen.

With every layer, truth laid bare,
We find ourselves in art laid bare.
A journey held in each detail,
In strokes of life, we weave our tale.

So let the colors freely flow,
In heart's embrace, let spirit grow.
For in this portrait, we shall see,
The beauty of what's meant to be.

Dance of Haunting Shadows

In twilight's grasp, they softly sway,
Shadows whisper secrets in dismay.
Each flicker tells a tale untold,
Of dreams long lost, of hearts grown cold.

Beneath the moon, they twirl and spin,
A ghostly dance, where none can win.
Echoes of laughter in the night,
Fading away with the dimming light.

They leap through memories, soft and light,
Brushing the edges of fading sight.
A spectral ball on the forest floor,
Where shadows gather, forevermore.

In shadows deep, they weave their art,
A tapestry woven from the heart.
Each swirl, each bend, a poignant song,
In the realm where both lost and strong belong.

As dawn approaches, the dance must cease,
The shadows blend, surrendering peace.
Yet in the silence, their echoes remain,
A haunting song of joy and pain.

The Gallery of Forgotten Affections

In dusty frames, their smiles decay,
Love letters tucked where dreams lay.
A canvas of whispers, shadowed light,
Stories of longing blink in the night.

Each portrait holds an untold tale,
Moments eclipsed, like a ship set sail.
Brushstrokes of yearning, thick with time,
Adorn the walls, a silent rhyme.

Old melodies twine through the air,
Resounding laughter, heart's sweet despair.
In every corner, a gentle sigh,
Echoes of love that once soared high.

Forgotten dreams line the gallery vast,
Treasures held tight, shadows are cast.
In every frame, a heartbeat waits,
For love to awaken, it hesitates.

Yet here they linger, etched in stone,
Silent witnesses, never alone.
In this gallery, past and present blend,
A testament to love that will never end.

Songs Carved in Time's Stone

From ancient lips, the melodies flow,
Echoes of life in their timeless glow.
Each note a memory, soft like a sigh,
Songs carved in stone that never die.

Whispers of ages drift on the breeze,
Carried through valleys, beneath the trees.
A chorus of hearts that beat as one,
Resounding through moonlight, 'til day is done.

With every heartbeat, the rhythm swells,
In the silence, a thousand tales dwell.
Every tear and laughter, intertwined,
In songs of the ages, forever enshrined.

As time wanders softly, we find our place,
In the symphony of life, we embrace.
A harmony formed from the trials we've known,
In songs carved in time's enduring stone.

And as the stars twinkle in the night,
We hum the tunes, our souls taking flight.
For deep in our hearts, we always must know,
The songs of our past will forever glow.

The Quietude of Inner Turmoil

In shadows deep, a tempest brews,
Whispers of doubt in haunted hues.
A calm facade drapes heavy and tight,
While storms of sorrow rage out of sight.

In silence's grip, the heart confides,
Unseen battles where chaos resides.
Each breath a struggle, a fragile plea,
Yearning for peace, but caught in the sea.

The echoes of voices, both soft and strong,
Demanding resolve to right the wrong.
In the quietude, pain finds its way,
As fears dance around from night into day.

Yet in the stillness, a flicker of light,
Hope weaves through shadows, dispelling the night.
From turmoil's depths, resilience will rise,
Transforming despair into painted skies.

So let the quiet embrace the storm,
For within the chaos, new shapes are born.
In the heart's turmoil, strength will emerge,
A symphony crafted from each quiet surge.

Whispers that Shatter the Stillness

In shadows deep where secrets hide,
A gentle breeze begins to glide.
Soft murmurs dance through quiet air,
Awakening dreams that linger there.

With every sigh, the stillness breaks,
As echoes of the night awake.
Voices of the past now call,
In whispers sweet, so faint, enthrall.

Moonlight weaves through branches bare,
Each shimmering thread a moment rare.
Stars above join in the plea,
To share their light, to set them free.

A heart once bound begins to soar,
Discovering realms unseen before.
With every note, a memory stirs,
In whispered tales, the soul concurs.

So let the whispers softly chase,
The stillness left in time and space.
For in their dance, a truth will bloom,
Unveiling life beyond the gloom.

The Canvas of Fleeting Moments

Brush strokes of gold on faded skies,
Moments captured with fleeting sighs.
Each hue a memory, bright and faint,
Turning whispers to the canvas quaint.

Time slows down in a painter's hand,
Colors mingle, taking a stand.
A touch of blue, a splash of red,
In every stroke, the past is fed.

Cascades of joy with shadows cast,
The palette pushing, shifting fast.
A sunset's warmth, a lover's glance,
In painted dreams, the heart finds dance.

Yet moments fade as daylight wanes,
Coinciding laughter, unseen pains.
The canvas waits with open grace,
For stories etched, a timeless trace.

With each brush stroke, time slips away,
Reminding us in its quiet play.
Hold tightly now to colors bright,
For fleeting moments bring pure light.

Threads of Light in Dark Waters

In waters deep, where shadows creep,
Threads of light begin to leap.
Glimmers dance on the surface still,
A gentle spark, a glowing thrill.

Beneath the waves, the secrets lie,
As currents whisper and shadows sigh.
With each soft pulse, they weave their tale,
Of hopes and dreams that take the sail.

Emerging bright from depths unknown,
A tapestry of light is sewn.
Through darkened paths, they find their way,
Unraveling fears, come what may.

In every ripple, a story spins,
Of battles fought, of losses, wins.
Threads entwined in a shadowed dance,
Leading to a second chance.

So let the light in dark waters stay,
To guide us through the night and fray.
For in the depths, hope starts to gleam,
Creating ripples in life's dream.

Pulse of Heartstrings

With every beat, a whisper flows,
Through heartstrings taut, the music grows.
Harmony echoes in breaths we take,
A symphony in the calm we make.

Emotions surge like rising tides,
As love ignites, the heart abides.
In every pause, a sacred space,
Where silence dwells, a warm embrace.

Rhythms dance, in sync, entwined,
In pulses soft, our souls aligned.
A gentle thrum beneath the skin,
A pulse of life where dreams begin.

Steady beats through the stormy night,
A beacon's glow, a guiding light.
Through laughter, tears, and joys we share,
The pulse of heartstrings, forever rare.

So let us listen to love's refrain,
As heartstrings vibrate through pleasure and pain.
For in their song, our spirits rise,
In life's grand symphony, together we fly.

Labyrinths of Lingering Thoughts

In shadows deep, my mind does roam,
Through winding paths, I seek a home.
Each twist reveals another fear,
Lost in the maze, where time feels queer.

Whispers echo, soft and low,
Memories dance like falling snow.
The walls close in, yet space expands,
A puzzle formed by unseen hands.

Fragments of dreams float in the air,
A lingering touch, a silent stare.
With every step, I tread on glass,
Hoping to find what shadows pass.

Beneath each turn, a tale untold,
A heart once young, now weary and old.
Yet in the dark, a glimmer shines,
A thread of hope, through tangled lines.

So I wander, though lost I seem,
Chasing echoes of a forgotten dream.
With every breath, I weave and spin,
Through labyrinths where thoughts begin.

The Cadence of a Broken Heart

In silence thick, a heart does ache,
Each beat a rhythm, a painful quake.
Memories linger, like shadows cast,
A fleeting love, now but a past.

The tears that fall are notes of woe,
A symphony played on strings of low.
Lost in a melody, harsh yet sweet,
Dancing alone, with empty feet.

In corners dark, where dreams now hide,
Emotions clash, collide, and bide.
Fragments break, like glass in flight,
Shattered echoes in the night.

Yet in the pain, a lesson learned,
From ashes cold, a fire burned.
A heart that's cracked knows how to mend,
Finding strength in every bend.

So I lift my voice, embrace the sting,
For every end brings forth a spring.
The cadence flows, though fractured art,
A music born from a broken heart.

Silence that Roars Within

In the quiet, a thunder grows,
Each heartbeat, a silent prose.
Conversations swirl in empty air,
Whispers of feelings too deep to share.

A storm brews in the depths of mind,
Words unspoken, love left behind.
The echoes reverberate, hauntingly clear,
Each soft sigh, a cry of fear.

Within the hush, the chaos lies,
A tempest raging without disguise.
Lingering doubts, like shadows creep,
Awake in silence, no chance for sleep.

Yet amidst the roar, a calm can breathe,
A fragile hope that takes its leave.
In quiet moments, strength can find,
A way to heal the weary mind.

So let the silence roar and swell,
Embrace the stories it knows so well.
For in the depths where whispers dwell,
Lies courage wrapped in a shroud of spell.

The Tapestry of Echoing Emotions

Stitches of joy, woven with tears,
A fabric rich, stitched through the years.
Colors blend in a vibrant hue,
Every thread tells stories true.

In moments muted, brightness unfolds,
In laughter shared, life's warmth beholds.
Tangles form where love has sown,
Yet beauty lies in the unknown.

Each layer thick, a history spun,
The fabric of life, a work begun.
Emotions dance in intricate lines,
Binding hearts in soft designs.

Through every tear, the light will thread,
Creating patterns of what is said.
Together woven, we stand, we fall,
A collective art, an eternal wall.

So behold the tapestry, grand and vast,
Of echoing emotions that forever last.
In every pain, a color shines,
A masterpiece formed from fragile lines.

Murmurs Under the Moonlit Sky

In shadows deep, whispers play,
Voices dance where night turns gray.
Stars above a glimmering sea,
Secrets shared with hushed decree.

Breeze carries tales from long ago,
In moonlight's glow, soft stories flow.
Every leaf, a silent friend,
Underneath the night's commend.

Gentle sighs in the cool night air,
Echoes of dreams, tender and rare.
With every blink, time holds its breath,
Murmurs linger, defying death.

Waves of thoughts like rivers stream,
In the quiet, we dare to dream.
Together we weave a silver thread,
In darkness deep, where angels tread.

So let us share, beneath the sky,
A love that soars, will never die.
In night's embrace, let shadows bind,
Murmurs whisper, hearts entwined.

Tidal Waves of Nostalgic Sighs

On shores of time, memories swell,
Waves of echoes, we know so well.
Each crash of tide brings thoughts of yore,
Tales of laughter and love we bore.

Seagulls cry, a bittersweet sound,
As footprints fade on hallowed ground.
With every pulse, the heart does bleed,
Yearning for moments, lost but freed.

Time's gentle hand brushes our face,
Guiding us through this endless space.
Every wave churns a secret tale,
Of warmth and joy, of love's soft veil.

Shells of memory lie in the sand,
Each a token of what we planned.
Tidal waves pull, then softly push,
Through the longing and quiet hush.

So let us stand, as waves resound,
In the crashing, our hearts are found.
With every sigh, a wish takes flight,
Tidal waves bring us back to light.

The Lullaby of Lost Moments

In twilight's hush, sweet dreams unfold,
A lullaby of tales retold.
Whispers float on velvet air,
Softly cradling joys laid bare.

Each moment drifts like autumn leaves,
In tangled branches, memory weaves.
Fleeting glances, a stolen kiss,
In shadows where we find our bliss.

Time slips by, a gentle thief,
Stealing hours, leaving grief.
Yet in the night, we hold them dear,
Lost moments, forever near.

Softly sung under stars so bright,
The lullaby fades into the night.
But in our hearts, the songs remain,
Harmonies born from joy and pain.

So let us listen, through every tear,
The lullaby draws us ever near.
In the stillness, let love abound,
In lost moments, our souls are found.

Chasing the Footsteps of Feelings

In the quiet dawn, where shadows blend,
Footsteps echo, around each bend.
Chasing whispers through morning dew,
A journey deep, to feelings true.

With every step, our hearts align,
Tracing paths where you were mine.
Golden rays pierce the gentle mist,
In the softness, memories twist.

Through fields of dreams, we walk in grace,
In each heartbeat, we find our place.
The air is thick with unspoken vows,
In the silence, love gently bows.

With every breath, we seek and find,
The footprints left by hearts entwined.
Lost in echoes of what once was,
Chasing feelings, without pause.

So here we stand, where time stands still,
In the embrace of a mutual thrill.
With every moment, love's sweet song,
In chasing footsteps, we belong.

Lullabies of a Weary Soul

In twilight's hush, soft whispers call,
Embracing dreams where shadows fall.
Gentle sighs on night's cool breath,
A song to dance with whispered death.

Moonlit rays through window gleam,
Cradle hearts in a tender dream.
Stars above, their vigil keep,
While weary souls drift into sleep.

A lullaby to ease the mind,
A sweet release from ties that bind.
Floating softly on silent tides,
Where hope and sorrow gently bide.

The world outside fades into gray,
As peace descends to softly sway.
In the arms of night, we find,
The gentle lull of love unlined.

Let weariness find its gentle rest,
In dreams where weary souls are blessed.
Each note of calm, a healing sound,
In lullabies, true solace found.

The Color of Sorrow's Light

In shades of blue, the shadows blend,
A canvas drawn where sorrows mend.
Brush strokes dance in soft despair,
As grief spills out in muted air.

Golden flecks through darkened skies,
Illuminate the pain that lies.
Each hue a tale, a tear's embrace,
A fleeting glimpse of hope's sweet face.

Emerald dreams on twilight's floor,
Whisper tales of love once more.
Fleeting laughter lost in streams,
Where every color softly gleams.

Through the prism, light refracts,
A testament to love's exact.
In sorrow's light, we learn to see,
The vibrant shades of memory.

Each stroke a journey, each shade a sigh,
Reflections linger 'neath the sky.
In colorful sorrow, we ignite,
The beauty found in darkest night.

When Tears Become Symphonies

In silence, tears begin to flow,
A melody from depths below.
Each drop a note that plays a score,
A symphony of grief, yet more.

Soft crescendos rise and fall,
Eloquent whispers, a lovers' call.
In harmony, each sorrowed sigh,
Transforms the night to a heartfelt cry.

With every tear, a story blooms,
In moonlit hush, where silence looms.
The opus builds, a heartfelt tale,
As sorrowed hearts begin to sail.

Through shattered dreams, the music weaves,
A tapestry of love that grieves.
And in that space, we find the way,
To turn our pain to notes at play.

When tears cascade, they find their tune,
An urgent dance beneath the moon.
A symphony of loss and grace,
Where beauty thrives in dark's embrace.

Breathing Life into Silent Grief

In quiet corners, shadows creep,
Where memories linger, lost in sleep.
With every breath, we feel the weight,
Of silent grief we cannot sate.

Yet in the stillness, whispers bloom,
As echoes rise from empty rooms.
Each sigh a plea for light to break,
To find the strength that we can make.

In fragile moments, courage wakes,
As hearts unite with every ache.
Breathing deeply, pain transforms,
Into a light that love reforms.

Hope dances through the veils of night,
Breathing life into our plight.
From ashes cold, new warmth we find,
As silent grief uncurls, unbinds.

Together, we embrace the strife,
As shadows fade, we spark new life.
With every breath, we heal the seams,
Breathing life into our dreams.

The Interlude of Unraveled Dreams

In shadows soft, the dreams take flight,
Whispered secrets in the night.
Threads of hope, unraveled seams,
A tapestry of shattered dreams.

Stars align and gently fade,
Lost in moments, time cascades.
Yet through the dark, a glow ignites,
Resilience born from endless nights.

Awake to find what lies ahead,
A heart reborn from ashes shed.
In every heartbeat, every sigh,
A testament, we still can fly.

Embrace the dawn with open arms,
For every ending, new charms.
In the silence, hear the calls,
An interlude where hope enthralls.

So weave your dreams, let fears unbind,
In the vast unknown, be kind.
For life's a dance, a fleeting breeze,
An interlude to set you free.

A Collection of Heartfelt Resounds

In gentle whispers, love's refrain,
Resounds through heart, through joy and pain.
Each note a memory, sweetly sung,
A collection of the hearts that clung.

Through laughter shared and tears we weep,
In every promise, secrets keep.
These echoes hold the warmth of light,
Guiding souls through starry night.

With every heartbeat, tales are spun,
Of battles lost, and victories won.
An album filled with colors bright,
A collection that feels just right.

Let words be gifts wrapped with care,
In quiet corners, love laid bare.
For every heartbeat, every sound,
A story in this space profound.

So hear the resounds, let them flow,
For in their cadence, we shall grow.
A heartfelt melody, our bond,
Through time and space, forever fond.

Triads of Time and Emotion

In triads formed of joy and strife,
Layers deep, this dance of life.
Moments blend, like colors splashed,
On canvas bright, time ever cast.

With every heartbeat, tales unfold,
Of love that's warm and dreams that bold.
In laughter shared, in tears we find,
The essence of a heart entwined.

Shadows stretch and fade away,
As memories and dreams hold sway.
In time's embrace, emotions bloom,
In fleeting moments, life resumes.

Thus journeys taken, paths have crossed,
In all we gain, in what we've lost.
These triads weave the fabric grand,
Of human tales across the land.

So hold these threads, let them unite,
In this tapestry of night.
For every laugh, every sigh,
Is a dance of time, a spirit high.

The Frequency of Fading Echoes

In whispered tones, the echoes call,
Resonating through the hall.
A frequency that drifts and sways,
Through countless nights and endless days.

As footsteps fade on dusty ground,
In memories, their voice is found.
The rhythm of the past still plays,
In hearts that beat in myriad ways.

For every silence, every sigh,
The echoes linger, never die.
They shape the tales we hold so dear,
In every shadow, every tear.

Yet as they fade, we find our song,
In changing tides, we still belong.
We dance within this timeless flow,
The frequency of what we know.

In every note, a story's spun,
A tapestry of hearts as one.
Though echoes fade into the night,
Their melody remains a light.

Whispers of the Heart's Reverberation

In quiet moments, feelings bloom,
Soft vibrations dispel the gloom.
A silent echo, gentle and true,
Whispers of love in shades of blue.

Held close within the beating chest,
Every heartbeat speaks of rest.
In twilight's grasp, secrets unfold,
A story of warmth, tender and bold.

As stars ignite the velvet sky,
With quiet sighs, we learn to fly.
In dreams we dance, two souls entwined,
The heart's reverberation, perfectly aligned.

Through subtle gestures, bonds are made,
In the depths of night, fears allayed.
An embrace that lingers, soft and light,
Guiding us through the endless night.

Let the whispers be our guide,
In every shadow where love does hide.
For in the silence, truths are spun,
The melody of two, forever one.

Shadows of Silent Longing

In the twilight, shadows play,
Silent whispers drift away.
Yearning hearts, a gentle ache,
Longing for the bonds we make.

Through haunted halls, echoes roam,
In the darkness, seek a home.
The heartbeat of a distant thought,
The warmth of love that time forgot.

Secrets linger in the air,
In every moment, a longing stare.
Each sigh is steeped in muted grace,
Tracing memories we can't erase.

Yet in the void, a flicker glows,
In silence, a deeper truth shows.
For shadows deepen, but hearts will strive,
In silent longing, love survives.

Beneath the moon's soft, silver sheen,
A tapestry of dreams unseen.
Together still, through storm and night,
The shadows fade before the light.

Reflections in the Rain

Pattering softly, droplets fall,
On windowpanes, they dance and call.
Mirrors of yearning, stories shared,
Reflections of love, tenderly bared.

Each splash a memory, sweet and rare,
Captured moments in the chilly air.
In every puddle, dreams collide,
A world of wonders we cannot hide.

Through each drop, a glimpse of grace,
The heart finds solace in this space.
Beneath the gray, the colors play,
As hope and joy bloom in disarray.

Time flows onward, like streams of light,
Yet in the rain, our spirits unite.
With every heartbeat, the world transforms,
In reflections, love's essence warms.

So let it rain, let the heart pour,
In every echo, we find the core.
For through the storm, we come alive,
In reflections, our dreams survive.

Traces of Forgotten Laughter

In autumn's breeze, laughter lingers,
Echoes dancing on outstretched fingers.
Faded whispers in rustling leaves,
Traces of joy the heart believes.

Through sunlit days and moonlit nights,
Memories shimmer in fading sights.
A playful tease, a gentle joke,
Moments captured, softly spoke.

In every giggle, a tale unfolds,
Stories woven in youthful gold.
Years may pass and shadows grow,
Yet laughter's trace will always flow.

The bonds we share, a vibrant thread,
In laughter's echo, love is spread.
So let us cherish each blissful sound,
In the heart's embrace, where joy is found.

With every chuckle, a spark remains,
Reminding us of loves gained and pains.
For in the laughter, life reveals,
Traces of joy that time conceals.

Flashes of Flickering Hope

In shadows cast by doubt's grip,
A spark ignites with a gentle slip.
Through darkened times, a glimmer grows,
Whispers of light where courage flows.

Resilient hearts dare to believe,
In moments bright, we can perceive.
A beacon shines amidst the pain,
Each flicker speaks of hope's refrain.

Though storms may rage and winds may howl,
We stand our ground; we will not cowl.
Together, we chase the fading night,
In each small spark, we find our flight.

With every dawn that breaks anew,
We grab the dreams that we pursue.
In flashes bright, we'll find our way,
Through flickering hope, we greet the day.

So hold on tight to that small light,
Let it guide you through the night.
In unity, let spirits soar,
For hope's a flame forevermore.

The Weave of Wistful Reminiscence

In threads of time, we weave our tales,
With echoes soft in gentle gales.
Each moment captured, sweetly spun,
A tapestry where dreams have run.

Through golden hues of yesteryear,
We find the joys and shed a tear.
In whispers low, the past will sing,
A symphony of everything.

With every knot, a story stays,
In muted colors of our days.
Our laughter lingers in the air,
The weave of time, a fragrant care.

As memories drift like autumn leaves,
In every heart, a joy believes.
The ties of love that bind us tight,
Illuminate the softest night.

So cherish well each tender thread,
For in this weave, the heart is fed.
Wistful dreams that dance and flow,
In memories rich, the shadows glow.

Poets of the Heart's Landscape

In meadows wide, where feelings bloom,
The poets carve their gentle loom.
Each word a petal, soft and clear,
A voice that whispers, drawing near.

Through valleys deep and mountains high,
Their verses soar, a melody.
With every line, a truth unfolds,
A glimpse of life that love beholds.

In twilight's glow, the starlit skies,
The poets speak, where beauty lies.
In every heart, a canvas spreads,
With strokes of ink, their vision leads.

A sonnet here, a ballad there,
They craft the world with utmost care.
Through laughter, tears, they bravely tread,
The landscape blooms, where dreams are bred.

With every verse, we find a home,
In scribbled thoughts, we dare to roam.
With poets brave, our hearts align,
In the landscape rich, our souls entwine.

Lanterns in the Fog of Recall

In foggy paths where shadows chase,
The lanterns glow, a soft embrace.
They flicker bright, through memories lost,
A guiding light, no matter the cost.

With every step, the haze may swell,
Yet in our hearts, those lanterns dwell.
They pierce the gloom, with warmth and grace,
Illuminating each hidden face.

In whispered tales of yesteryears,
The lanterns shed their tender tears.
With stories shared and laughter bright,
They light the corners of the night.

Though time may fade and days grow dim,
The lanterns burn, we'll not grow grim.
For in recall, we find our strength,
In memories held, we find our length.

So take a breath, let shadows part,
The lanterns guide the wandering heart.
Through fog and mist, we'll find our way,
To brighter shores, where hope can play.

In the Whisper of Warmth

In shadows where the light softly glows,
Whispers of warmth in the evening flows.
Embers dance like memories set free,
Comforting tales of what's meant to be.

Stars ignite in the velvet night sky,
Each twinkle a wish, a soft lullaby.
Hearts beat in rhythm, as time takes a pause,
In the whisper of warmth, love gently draws.

Gentle breezes carry the scent of the past,
Moments like treasures, forever to last.
Wrapped in the silence, the night hums a tune,
In the whisper of warmth, we swoon by the moon.

Candles flicker with secrets to share,
Encircled by shadows, we breathe in the air.
Every heartbeat whispers, every sigh a prayer,
In the whisper of warmth, we find solace there.

Time melts like wax, drips soft on the floor,
Memory's touch opens a hidden door.
In the stillness, love's promise is sworn,
In the whisper of warmth, we are reborn.

The Storm Before the Calm

Dark clouds gather, a whisper of dread,
Nature's fury in silence is fed.
Lightning strikes with a jagged shine,
In the storm's embrace, we learn to entwine.

Rain beats heavy on rooftops above,
Each drop carries pain, yet also love.
Chaos erupts, a dance wild and free,
In the storm's heart, we find unity.

Wind howls loud, a chorus of fears,
Together we face what's hidden in tears.
The tempest swirls, a fierce, wild trance,
Yet in its turmoil, we find our chance.

Through turmoil's grip, we seek the light,
After the storm, comes the dawn so bright.
With every thunder, the heart learns to scope,
The storm before calm, is a cradle of hope.

As skies start to clear, colors unfold,
The promise of peace in hues bright and bold.
From tempest to stillness, we learn to embrace,
The storm before calm leaves a lasting trace.

The Fabric of Unexpressed Dreams

Threads of silence weave through the night,
Inquiet whispers that take flight.
Colors of longing, shades of despair,
The fabric of dreams is woven with care.

Sewn with hopes that dare to be real,
Stitches of moments we wish to feel.
Gathered in shadows, they softly gleam,
The fabric of dreams is sewn with a seam.

Patterns unfold, like stars in the mind,
Invisible journeys we struggle to find.
Tangled and twisted, yet still they cling,
The fabric of dreams, a song yet to sing.

Each thread tells a tale of what could have been,
In the quiet corners where we have been.
Bound by our wishes, they silently flow,
The fabric of dreams through the heart's undertow.

As night turns to day, they'll glow in the light,
Their whispers of courage a powerful sight.
In every small heartbeat, each sigh and scream,
The fabric of dreams ignites the unseen.

Secrets Written in the Sand

Along the shore where the waves gently sigh,
Secrets lay buried beneath the sky.
Each grain a story, each tide a new hand,
Writing the past in the soft, shifting sand.

Footprints left in patterns of fleeting grace,
Echoes of laughter, they vanish without trace.
Whispers of wishes upon salty breeze,
Secrets written in sand, carried with ease.

The ocean keeps tales of love and of loss,
Each wave a reminder of the paths we cross.
Fleeting as clouds that dance overhead,
Secrets written in sand, softly fled.

In twilight's embrace, stories take flight,
Beneath the pink glow, the world feels so right.
The moonlight unveils the tales in the dark,
Secrets written in sand, a timeless spark.

As the tides rise, we watch what's concealed,
Nature's canvas, secrets revealed.
With every new dawn, they blend and expand,
Secrets forever written in the sand.

Milton Keynes UK
Ingram Content Group UK Ltd.
UKHW022049111124
451035UK00014B/1023

9 789916 866122